BLAZERS

Teeth, Claws, and Jaws:

ANIMAL WEAPONS AND DEFENSES

BY JANET RIEHECKY

CONTENT CONSULTANT:
JACKIE GAI, DVM
ZOO AND EXOTIC ANIMAL VETERINARIAN

READING CONSULTANT:
BARBARA J. FOX
READING SPECIALIST
PROFESSOR EMERITUS
NORTH CAROLINA STATE UNIVERSITY

CAPSTONE PRESS
a capstone imprint

Blazers is published by Capstone Press,
1710 Roe Crest Drive, North Mankato, Minnesota 56003.
www.capstonepub.com

Books published by Capstone Press are manufactured with paper
containing at least 10 percent post-consumer waste.

Library of Congress Cataloging-in-Publication Data
Riehecky, Janet, 1953–
    Teeth, claws, and jaws: animal weapons and defenses / by Janet Riehecky.
    p. cm. — (Blazers. animal weapons and defenses)
    Includes bibliographical references and index.
    Summary: "Describes how animals use teeth, claws, and jaws as weapons and defenses"
—Provided by publisher.
    ISBN 978-1-4296-6506-3 (library binding)
    ISBN 978-1-4296-8012-7 (paperback)
    1. Teeth—Juvenile literature. 2. Claws—Juvenile literature. 3. Jaws—Juvenile literature.
I. Title.
QL858.R54 2012
599.9'43—dc23   2011034683

Editorial Credits
Mandy Robbins, editor; Kyle Grenz, designer; Svetlana Zhurkin, media researcher;
    Laura Manthe, production specialist

Photo Credits
Alamy: FLPA, 24–25; Corbis: John Madere, 10–11; Dreamstime: John Anderson, 28–29,
Photomyeye, 16–17, Richard Lowthian, 26–27; Newscom: Getty Images/AFP/Greg Wood, 20–21;
PhotoAlto, 22–23; Photolibrary: Sylvain Cordier, 8–9; Shutterstock: Albie Venter, 14–15, Colin
Edwards Photography, cover (top), Eduard Kyslynskyy, 6–7, Four Oaks, 18–19, Johan Swanepoel,
4–5, Phillip W. Kirkland, 12–13, wcpmedia, cover (bottom)

Printed in the United States of America in
Stevens Point, Wisconsin.
102011   006404WZS12

TABLE of CONTENTS

GETTING THE JOB DONE

Animals have two important jobs. First, they need to eat. Second, they must protect themselves from getting eaten. Sharp teeth, powerful jaws, and mighty claws help many animals do both.

SHARP TEETH

A tiger has four sharp **canine** teeth.

These teeth slice through **prey** like knives.

A tiger often kills by biting an animal's throat.

☆ FIERCE FACT ☆

A tiger can eat 65 pounds (29 kilograms) of meat in one meal. Then the tiger will often go days without eating.

canine—a long, pointed tooth

prey—an animal hunted by another animal for food

Packs of wolves chase down prey.

They bite at the animal's feet and sides.

When the animal falls, the wolves dig

in with sharp teeth.

pack—a small group of animals that hunt together

Piranhas use razor-sharp teeth to bite off chunks of flesh from other fish. Then they swallow without chewing.

★ FIERCE FACT ★

When piranhas close their mouths, their pointed top and bottom teeth fit together perfectly.

An opossum has 50 piercing teeth. These **mammals** play dead when they are first threatened. But they become fierce when attacked. Their sharp teeth slice through skin and bone.

An opossum has more teeth than any other mammal in North America.

mammal—a warm-blooded animal that has a backbone and feeds milk to its young

POWERFUL JAWS

Strong jaws help packs of hyenas attack zebras and antelope. A hyena's strong jaws bite with more force than a lion or a tiger. Hyenas even chew thick bones.

☆ **FIERCE FACT** ☆

A pack of hyenas can eat an entire zebra in 15 minutes.

Great white sharks have huge jaws lined with rows of serrated teeth. Just one big bite can finish off prey.

★ FIERCE FACT ★

When a great white shark attacks, it rolls its eyes back. Doing this protects the shark's eyes from struggling prey.

serrated—saw-toothed

Crocodiles snap up mammals, birds, and fish. They drive their teeth deep into prey. Large, strong jaws help crocodiles eat all of their prey, even the bones.

☆ FIERCE FACT ☆

Crocodiles are more likely to avoid people than attack them.

The Tasmanian devil is the biggest marsupial meat-eater. It eats almost everything, from insects to small animals. When a Tasmanian devil's jaws snap shut, it chomps through flesh and bone.

marsupial—a warm-blooded animal that carries its babies in a pouch

MIGHTY CLAWS

A leopard uses strong claws to drag its prey up into trees. There a leopard can feast on prey without other animals trying to steal a meal.

A leopard's long, razor-sharp claws slash through fur and skin.

Giant anteaters have no teeth, but their long, sharp claws make up for that. They tear into anthills and termite mounds. Then anteaters suck up a lunch of bugs.

An anteater flicks its tongue up to 160 times per minute as it slurps up bugs.

Eagles swoop out of the sky and sink their talons into prey. An eagle squeezes its talons tightly around prey to kill it. Eagles also use their talons to carry prey as they fly through the air.

★ FIERCE FACT ★

A bald eagle's wingspan is about 6 feet (2 meters).

talon—an eagle's claw; a talon has four toes, each with a very sharp, curved nail

A mantis shrimp uses two long claws to smash or stab prey. These claws are usually folded against its body. When prey swims by, the claws spring out.

☆ FIERCE FACT ☆

The strike of some mantis shrimp can break glass.

GLOSSARY

canine (KAY-nyn)—a long, pointed tooth

mammal (MAM-uhl)—a warm-blooded animal that has a backbone and feeds milk to its young

marsupial (mar-SOO-pee-uhl)—an animal that carries its young in a pouch

pack (PAK)—a small group of animals that hunts together

prey (PRAY)—an animal hunted by another animal for food

serrated (SER-ay-tid)—saw-toothed

talon (TAL-uhn)—an eagle's claw; a talon has four toes, each with a very sharp, curved nail

★ READ MORE ★

Collard, Sneed B. III. *Teeth.* Watertown, Mass.: Charlesbridge, 2008.

Seidensticker, John and Susan Lumpkin. *Predators.* Insiders. New York: Simon & Schuster Books for Young Readers, 2008.

Spada, Ada. *Fangs, Claws & Talons: Animal Predators.* Predatory Animals. New York: Lark Books, 2007.

INTERNET SITES

FactHound offers a safe, fun way to find Internet sites related to this book. All of the sites on FactHound have been researched by our staff.

Here's all you do:

Visit *www.facthound.com*

Type in this code: 9781429665063

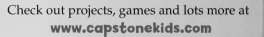

Super-cool stuff! Check out projects, games and lots more at
www.capstonekids.com

INDEX